LEADER'S GUIDE

DISCOVERING GOD'S WAY OF HANDLING MONEY

Video Series

CROWN FINANCIAL MINISTRIES
Crown.org

CONTENTS

CHAPTER

    What the Leader Needs to Know   4

1   Introduction   7

2   Debt   15

3   Counsel   23

4   Honesty   31

5   Giving   39

6   Work   47

7   Saving and Investing   53

8   Children   65

    Prayer Requests   71

Thank you for your willingness to help others discover God's way of handling money. It requires a commitment of time and effort to lead this video series, and we are grateful. You may be surprised to learn that the Lord said a lot about finances. There are more than 2,350 verses in the Bible that deal with money and possessions.

Our prayer is that your faithfulness in leadership will be rewarded as you encourage others to discover and apply God's practical and life-changing financial principles.

WHAT THE LEADER NEEDS TO KNOW

The *Discovering God's Way of Handling Money* video series contains 8 segments. Each addresses a different subject and is about 20 minutes long. Two videos (volume 1 and volume 2) contain 4 segments each. This video series may be used in a Sunday school class, weekend seminar or in other settings.

COURSE WORKBOOK

A Course Workbook, which should be used by each student or couple, has been designed to help students apply the principles they are learning.

 In the VIDEO NOTES section of each chapter there is an outline containing blank spaces for the students to fill-in key words. In order to help the students identify these words they appear in red on the video.

 The DISCUSSION QUESTIONS for each of the video sessions are designed to help your students personalize the content of each lesson. You can move to these questions immediately after the conclusion of the video.

 For those who wish to better grasp and apply the principles, there is an optional DIG DEEPER AND LEARN MORE section. In this portion of the Course Workbook there is a SCRIPTURE TO MEMORIZE, selected verses to look up, questions to answer, and a PRACTICAL EXERCISE TO COMPLETE.

 Before you end your class you may want to take PRAYER REQUESTS and record these in the back of the Course Workbook.

LEADER'S GUIDE

This Leader's Guide is divided into three sections: (1) What the leader needs to know, (2) A guide for each chapter, and (3) Prayer requests.

The chapter guides contain the key words to be filled-in and brief answers to the Discussion Questions. The leader will not need to use the Course Workbook —everything needed is in the Leader's Guide. There is a blank space following the Video Notes and Discussion Questions icons. To assist in monitoring the time so the class will end punctually, the leader may fill-in these spaces with the scheduled time for these items.

OTHER CROWN STUDIES AND MATERIALS

The video series is part of a comprehensive program that Crown Financial Ministries has developed to train people of all ages to handle money God's way. During the video series we will refer to the Crown Small Group Study for adults which is outstanding. We hope that you will encourage your students to enroll in it soon.

Other materials and studies are described in the Leader's Guide and Course Workbook and may be ordered from Crown Financial Ministries by calling 1-800-722-1976 or by visiting Crown's website at www.crown.org.

LEADER'S RESPONSIBILITIES

1. **Love and encourage.** The primary responsibility of the leader is to love and encourage the students. People are more receptive to spiritual truth when they have been loved. People want to know how much a leader cares before they care how much the leader knows.

2. **Let the video teachers teach**. Crown has worked hard at presenting the financial principles found in God's Word just so you don't have to. That means you can sit back and relax while the material is presented. Your expertise is needed *in facilitating and cultivating* good conversation during the discussion time.

3. **Understand group dynamics**. The most effective discussions involve group interaction. The leader shouldn't do all the talking. The leader should facilitate the discussion and establish an environment in which students have the freedom to express insights and questions.

GETTING STARTED

Several ingredients are essential to any successful group study. Before the first meeting, you should.

1. **Pray!** Only God can change the hearts of people, and prayer is your most powerful tool.

2. **Organize**. Consider asking one or two others to share the leadership load by helping you plan, promote the series, distribute materials, etc.

3. **Order the Course Workbooks**. Before starting the course, make sure that each participant has his or her own copy of the Course Workbook. You may want to have extra copies on hand to accommodate late additions. If your sponsoring organization is not underwriting the cost of materials, then consider structuring your class so that the Course Workbook is part of a registration fee.

4. **Prepare to lead the sessions**. View the video segment, complete the Discussion Questions and the Dig Deeper and Learn More section before class meets. This will help you understand the content and better facilitate the discussion.

LEADING THE CLASS

1. **Prayer**. We recommend that you start the class with prayer, and end it with prayer. Remember, only the Lord can change lives.

2. **Be yourself**. The others in your group will appreciate and follow your example of openness and honesty as you lead—so set a good example! When they sense that you are "real"—that you struggle with the same issues that challenge them—they will be encouraged.

3. **Structure your time**. Whether you are leading this series in Sunday school, a weekend seminar, or other setting, you'll find the materials are ideal. The course is designed so that the video teaching and the discussion questions can be completed in 45 minutes per chapter.

4. **Outside of Class**. It is wise for the leader to contact the students outside of class by phone, letter, e-mail or a personal visit to express your appreciation for their participation. Demonstrating your care for the students will encourage them to apply these principles.

CHAPTER ONE

INTRODUCTION

"Everything in the heavens and the earth is yours, O Lord."
1 Chronicles 29:11, LB

DAVID
Worshiping the Lord at the dedication
of the offering for the temple.

M ANY PEOPLE ARE EXPERIENCING FINANCIAL CHALLENGES. They are facing growing debt, little or no savings, inadequate income, and no plans for their financial future. Surveys reveal that more than half of all divorces are a result of financial tension in the home.

Others are financially sound, but suffocating materialism has robbed them of their spiritual vitality. They are not spending their resources in eternally significant ways.

Fortunately, the Bible has the answers to these financial difficulties—it contains more than 2,350 verses dealing with money and possessions. In fact, Jesus Christ said more about money than almost any other subject. Financial matters are addressed throughout Scripture for both spiritual and practical reasons.

 **VIDEO NOTES** _____

WHY THE LORD SAYS SO MUCH ABOUT MONEY

1. Spiritual Reasons
How we handle money has a significant impact on the _____ intimacy _____ of our relationship with Christ.

> *"If therefore you are not faithful in the use of worldly wealth, who will entrust the true riches to you"* (Luke 16:11).

Money is a primary competitor with Christ for the _____ lordship _____ of our life.

> *"No one can serve two masters; for either he will hate the one and love the other . . . You cannot serve God and money"* (Matthew 6:24).

2. Practical Reasons
The Lord wanted to give us a blueprint for handling our money. Scripture gives us clear principles for earning, spending, saving, investing, giving, getting out of debt, and teaching our children how to handle money.

The financial practices of most people are in sharp _____ contrast _____ to the principles of scripture.

> *"For My thoughts are not your thoughts, neither are your ways My ways,"* declares the Lord. *"For as the heavens are higher than the earth, so are My ways higher than your ways and My thoughts than your thoughts"* (Isaiah 55:8-9).

GOD'S PART IN OUR FINANCES
Scripture teaches there are two distinct responsibilities in the handling of money: the part God plays and the part we play.

1. Ownership

God is the owner of everything. Psalm 24:1 reads, *"The earth is the Lord's, and all it contains."*

If we are going to be genuine followers of Christ, we must transfer the ownership of our possessions to the Lord (Luke 14:33).

The first step in learning _____contentment_____, is recognizing God is the owner of all your possessions.

2. Control

Our heavenly Father is in ultimate _____control_____ of every event.

> *"We adore you as being in control of everything"* (1 Chronicles 29:11, LB). *"I praised the Most High . . . He does as he pleases with the powers of heaven and the peoples of the earth. No one can hold back his hand or say to him: 'What have you done?'"* (Daniel 4:34).

It is comforting for the child of God to realize that his heavenly Father orchestrates even seemingly devastating circumstances for ultimate good.

> *"And we know that God causes _____all_____ _____things_____ to work together for good to those who love God, to those who are called according to His purpose"* (Romans 8:28).

3. Provision

The Lord promises to _____provide_____ for our needs. Jesus said, *"But seek first the kingdom of God, and his righteousness; and all these things (food and clothing) shall be added unto you"* (Matthew 6:33).

God is both _____predictable_____ and unpredictable. He is absolutely predictable in His faithfulness to provide. What we cannot predict is how the Lord will provide.

The basic reason most fail to recognize God's part is that we do not know who God really is. We tend to _____shrink_____ Him down to our own human abilities and limitations.

> *"You are _____familiar_____ with all my ways. Before a word is on my tongue you know it completely, O Lord"* (Psalm 139:3-4, NIV).

OUR PART

Our responsibility is that of a _____steward_____ or manager of the Lord's possessions.

Our responsibility is to be _____faithful_____ stewards.

> *"It is required in stewards, that a man be found faithful"*
> (1 Corinthians 4:2).

Most of us have not learned how to handle the other __90__ percent.

Faithful in little things.

> *"He who is faithful in a very little thing is faithful also in much; and he who is unrighteous in a very little thing is unrighteous also in much"*
> (Luke 16:10).

Small things are small things, but faithfulness with a _____small_____ thing is a _____big_____ thing.

DISCUSSION QUESTIONS _____
(TIME)

1. After viewing this Introduction section of the *Discovering God's Way of Handling Money* video series, describe the most important principle you learned.

2. How will applying this principle impact you?

3. This video series will address many financial issues from God's perspective, such as, earning, spending, saving, giving, investing, getting out of debt and teaching children how to handle money. What would be the one thing you want to happen as you learn and apply these principles?

 PRAYER REQUESTS (OPTIONAL)

DIG DEEPER AND LEARN MORE (OPTIONAL)

After each section, there are optional exercises you may do on your own that will help you learn and apply God's financial principles. There will be a scripture to memorize, some questions to answer and a helpful practical financial exercise to complete.

 SCRIPTURE TO MEMORIZE
"Everything in the heavens and earth is yours, O Lord, and this is your kingdom. We adore you as being in control of everything" (1 Chronicles 29:11, LB).

QUESTIONS TO ANSWER
List the specific items in these verses that the Lord owns.

Leviticus 25:23 — [God owns the land.]

Psalm 50:10-12 — [God owns the animals.]

Haggai 2:8 — [God owns all the gold and silver.]

Read *1 Chronicles 29:11*.

Do you consistently recognize the Lord as true owner of all your possessions? Give two practical suggestions that would help.

1. [Memorize *1 Chronicles 29:11* and meditate on it for 30 days.]

2. [Develop habits that will help you recognize God's ownership. For example, every time you spend money thank the Lord for his ownership.]

Read *Genesis 45:4-8* and *Romans 8:28.*

Why is it important to realize that God controls and uses even difficult circumstances for good in the life of a godly person?

> [God works every situation for good for those who love Him. Joseph is a example of a godly person who suffered difficult circumstances that God intended for ultimate good.]

How does this perspective impact you today?

 **PRACTICAL EXERCISE TO COMPLETE**

The Personal Financial Statement
Complete the personal financial statement on the next page to get a picture of your current financial situation. This is the first step in getting a grasp on your finances. It is not necessary to be precise to the penny; rather, estimate the value of each asset and the amount of each liability. We recommend that you revise your personal financial statement once a year to help you keep abreast of your progress.

PERSONAL FINANCIAL STATEMENT

Assets (Present market value)	
Cash on hand/Checking account	
Stocks and Bonds	
Cash value of life insurance	
Home	
Other real estate	
Mortgages / Notes receivable	
Business valuation	
Automobiles / vehicles	
Furniture	
Jewelry	
Other personal property	
IRA	
Pension / Retirement plan	
Other assets	
Total Assets	
Liabilities (Current amount owed)	
Credit card debt	
Automobile loans	
Home Mortgage	
Other real estate mortgages	
Personal debts to relatives	
Business loans	
Medical/Other past due bills	
Life insurance loans	
Bank loans	
Other debts and loans	
Total Liabilities	
Net Worth (total assets minus total liabilities):	

INTRODUCTION

CHAPTER TWO

DEBT

A godly woman finds herself in debt.
"My husband is dead . . . and the creditor has come
to take my two children to be his slaves."
2 Kings 4:1

DEBT HAS BECOME A WAY OF LIFE FOR MANY PEOPLE. PERSONAL consumer debt in our country increases at the rate of $1,000 per second.
We are drowning in a sea of debt, the average family spending $400 more than it earns each year. And with all this credit floating around, more and more people are declaring bankruptcy—more than one million individuals a year.

What is debt? The dictionary defines debt as: "Money which one person is obligated to pay to another." Debt includes money owed to credit card companies, bank loans, money borrowed from relatives, and the home mortgage. Bills that come due, such as the monthly electric bill, are not considered debt if they are paid on time.

VIDEO NOTES (TIME)

SCRIPTURE'S PERSPECTIVE ON DEBT

1. Debt Is Discouraged.

    "Owe no man any thing" (KJV). *"Pay all your* ___debts___ *"* (LB).
    "Owe nothing to anyone" (NAS). *"Keep out of debt and owe no man
    anything"* (Romans 13:8, AMPLIFIED).

2. Debt Is Slavery.

    "Just as the rich rule the poor, so the borrower is ___servant___ *to the
    lender"* (Proverbs 22:7).

3. Old Testament View of Debt.

    One of the rewards for ___obedience___ was being out of debt.

    *"If you will diligently obey the Lord your God . . . all these blessings shall
    come upon you . . . and you shall lend to many nations, but you shall not
    borrow"* (Deuteronomy 28:1-2,12).

    Debt was one of the ___curses___ for disobedience.

    *"If you will not obey the Lord your God . . . all these curses shall come
    upon you. . . . The alien who is among you shall rise above you higher and
    higher . . . He shall lend to you, but you shall not lend to him . . ."*
    (Deuteronomy 28:15, 43-44).

4. Scriptural Warning Against Presumption.

    *"Come now, you who say, 'Today or tomorrow, we shall go to such and such
    a city, and spend a year there and engage in business and make a profit.' Yet
    you do not know what your life will be like tomorrow. . . . Instead, you
    ought to say, 'If the Lord wills, we shall live and also do this or that'"*
    (James 4:13).

D E B T

When Can We Owe Money?

In our opinion, it is permissible to borrow for: (1) home mortgage, (2) your vocation or (3) your business.

The following three criteria must be met:

1. The item purchased produces and income or has the potential to appreciate.

2. The value of the item equals or exceeds the amount owed against it.

3. The debt is not so high that the repayment puts undue strain on the budget.

How to Get Out of Debt

1. Pray

2. Establish a written __budget__.

3. List your __assets__—everything you own. Determine if you should sell any assets and use that money toward debt reduction.

4. List your __liabilities__—everything you owe.

5. Establish a debt __repayment__ schedule.

Decide which debts to pay off first. Your decision should be based on two factors: the size of the debts and the interest rate charged.

6. Consider earning additional __income__.

7. Accumulate no __new__ debt.

8. Consider a radical change in your __lifestyle__.

9. Do not give up!

TYPES OF DEBT

1. Automobile Debt
Keep your car long enough to pay off your automobile loan. Then, continue paying the monthly car payment but into your own savings account.

2. Home Mortgage
If you have a home mortgage, seek the Lord's direction about paying it off more quickly than scheduled.

3. Investment Debt
In our opinion it is permissible to borrow for investments, but only if the investment for which you borrow is the sole collateral for the debt.

4. Business Debt

COSIGNING
A person who cosigns becomes legally ____responsible____ for the debt of another.

> *"It is poor judgment to cosign another's note, to become responsible for his debts"* (Proverbs 17:18, LB).

DISCUSSION QUESTIONS _____
(TIME)

1. Why do you think so many people in our country are in debt?

2. How does the Lord view debt?

3. Do you have a strategy to get out of debt? If you have a plan, describe it.

PRAYER REQUESTS (OPTIONAL)

DIG DEEPER AND LEARN MORE (OPTIONAL)

QUESTIONS TO ANSWER

Read *2 Kings 4:1-7*. What principles of getting out of debt can you identify from this passage?

> [Seek the counsel of godly people, use whatever assets you have, and involve the entire family.]

How can you apply any of these principles to your current situation?

Read *Proverbs 22:26-27*. What does this passage say about cosigning? How does this apply to you?

> [Do not cosign. If you do, you may loose assets you need.]

Read *Proverbs 6:1-5*. If someone has cosigned a loan, what should he or she attempt to do?

> [Diligently seek the release of the obligation.]

 **PRACTICAL EXERCISE TO COMPLETE**

The Debt List

Many people don't know precisely what they owe. The debt list will assist you in compiling your debts and the terms of each debt. The columns on the debt list are as follows:

Creditor — The one to whom the debt is owed.

Interest rate — The rate charged for the debt.

Monthly payment — The amount of the monthly payment. If payment is due more often than monthly, compute the total amount that is paid each month. For example, a $100 loan payment paid twice each month equals $200 per month. If payment is due less frequently, determine the average monthly cost.

Balance due — The amount of the outstanding balance.

DEBT LIST

Creditor	Interest Rate	Monthly Payment	Balance Due
	TOTALS		

DEBT

CHAPTER THREE

COUNSEL

"The way of a fool is right in his own eyes."
Proverbs 12:15

SOLOMON—
sought wisdom from a multitude
of counselors.

Many financial problems could be avoided if people would seek counsel before making the decisions that place them in financial jeopardy. Seeking godly counsel can help us avoid costly mistakes. This is in sharp contrast to our culture's practice that says: be a rugged individualist who makes decisions alone and unafraid, coping with any financial pressure in stoic silence.

King Solomon is most often remembered as the wisest king who has ever lived. In fact, he made wisdom a subject of study. In Proverbs he wrote, *"Wisdom is better than jewels; and all desirable things cannot compare with her"* (8:11). Solomon's practical recommendation for embracing wisdom is found in Proverbs, *"Listen to advice and accept instruction, and in the end you will be wise"* (19:20, NIV). Practice seeking counsel.

VIDEO NOTES _____

(TIME)

SCRIPTURE ENCOURAGES US TO SEEK COUNSEL

"The way of a fool is right in his own eyes, but a wise man is he who listens to _____counsel_____ *"* (Proverbs 12:15).

TWO ATTITUDES KEEP US FROM SEEKING COUNSEL

1. The attitude of _____pride_____.

2. The attitude of _____stubbornness_____.

SOURCES OF COUNSEL

1. The _____scriptures_____

   "Your laws are both my light and my _____counselors_____ " (Psalm 119:24).

   "For the Word of God is _____living_____ and active and sharper than any two-edged sword . . . and able to judge the thoughts and intentions of the heart" (Hebrews 4:12).

2. Godly _____ Men and Women

   "The godly man is a good counselor because he is just and fair and knows right from wrong" (Psalm 37:30-31, LB).

   Your _____spouse_____

   Your _____parents_____

   "My son, observe the commandment of your _____father_____ and do not forsake the teaching of your _____mother_____ (Proverbs 6:20-22).

   Multitude of counselors

   "Plans fail for lack of counsel, but with _____many_____ advisers they succeed" (Proverbs 15:22).

3. The Lord

"*Wonderful* ___counselor___ " (Isaiah 9:6).

We receive the counsel of the Lord by ___praying___ and ___listening___.

COUNSEL TO AVOID

"*How blessed is the man who does not walk in the counsel of the* ___wicked___ " (Psalm 1:1).

A wicked person is one who lives his or her life without regard to ___God___.

"*Do not turn to mediums or spiritists; do* ___not___ *seek them out to be defiled by them. I am the Lord your God*" (Leviticus 19:31).

DISCUSSION QUESTIONS ___
(TIME)

1. What are some of the benefits you have experienced from seeking counsel?

2. What hinders you from seeking counsel?

3. Read *Psalm 119:24; 2 Timothy 3:16-17* and *Hebrews 4:12*. What does this say to you about the Bible? Do you consistently read and study the Bible? If not, what prevents your consistency?

   [The Bible is living and provides direction for our lives.]

PRAYER REQUESTS (OPTIONAL)

DIG DEEPER AND LEARN MORE (OPTIONAL)

QUESTIONS TO ANSWER

1. Read *Psalm 16:7* and *Psalm 32:8*. Does the Lord actively counsel His children? How do you seek the Lord's counsel?

    [The Lord does counsel His children.]

2. Have you ever suffered for not seeking the Lord's counsel? If so, describe what happened.

3. If you are married, describe how you currently seek (or intend to seek) the counsel of your spouse.

PRACTICAL EXERCISE TO COMPLETE

FINANCIAL GOALS

Determining your financial goals will help you accomplish what is important to you. You will be better able to control and prioritize your spending with those goals in mind. If you are married, complete this with your spouse.

YOUR FINANCIAL GOALS

Giving Goals:

Would like to give _____ percent of my income.

Other giving goals:

Debt Repayment Goals:

Would like to pay off the following debts first:

CREDITOR	AMOUNT

Educational Goals:

Would like to fund the following education:

PERSON	SCHOOL	ANNUAL COST	TOTAL COST

Other educational goals:

continued

Lifestyle Goals:

Would like to make the following major purchases: (home, automobile, travel, and so forth)

ITEM	AMOUNT

Would like to achieve the following annual income: _____

Savings and Investing Goals:

Would like to save _____ percent of my income.

Other savings goals:

Would like to make the following investments:

INVESTMENT	AMOUNT

Would like to provide my heirs with the following:

Starting a Business:

 Would like to invest in or begin my/our own business:

Goals for this Year:

 I believe the Lord wants me/us to achieve the following goals this year:

PRIORITY	FINANCIAL GOALS	STEPS NEEDED TO ACHIEVE GOAL

CHAPTER FOUR

HONESTY

"You shall not steal, nor deal falsely, nor lie to one another."
Leviticus 19:11

DANIEL—
"They could find no ground of accusation or evidence of corruption, inasmuch as he was faithful . . ." **Daniel 6:4**

ALL OF US HAVE TO MAKE DAILY DECISIONS ABOUT WHETHER OR not to handle money honestly. Do we tell the cashier at the grocery store when we receive too much change? Have you ever been tempted to sell something and not tell the whole truth because you might lose the sale?

These decisions are made more difficult because everyone around seems to be acting dishonestly. However, the Lord has clearly established the standard of absolute honesty for His children. Hundreds of verses demand that we be people of integrity in the midst of a dishonest culture.

It often requires faith to make honest decisions. Consequently, the commitment to be honest in even the smallest things is one of the keys to growing deeper in your intimacy with Christ.

VIDEO NOTES (TIME)

PEOPLE FORMULATE STANDARDS OF HONESTY

"Everyone did whatever he wanted to, whatever seemed right in his own eyes" (Judges 17:6).

GOD DEMANDS ABSOLUTE HONESTY

"The Lord loathes all cheating and dishonesty" (Proverbs 20:23, LB).

"Lying lips are an abomination to the Lord" (Proverbs 12:22).

"You shall not ____steal____, nor deal falsely, nor lie to one another" (Leviticus 19:11).

Truthfulness is one of ____God's____ attributes. The Lord wants us to become conformed to His honest nature.

"Be holy yourselves also in all your behavior; because it is written, 'You shall be holy, for I am holy'" (1 Peter 1:15, 16).

WHY GOD HAS IMPOSED THE STANDARD OF ABSOLUTE HONESTY

1. We cannot practice dishonesty and ____love____ God.

"He who walks in his uprightness fears the Lord, but he who is crooked in his ways despises Him" (Proverbs 14:2).

Honest behavior is often an issue of ____faith____.

2. We cannot practice dishonesty and love our ____neighbor____.

"If you love your neighbor as much as you love yourself you will not want to harm or cheat him . . . or steal from him . . . love does no wrong to anyone" (Romans 13:9-10, LB).

3. Honesty creates credibility for _____evangelism_____.

> *"Prove yourselves to be blameless and innocent, children of God above reproach in the midst of a crooked and perverse generation, among whom you appear as lights in the world"* (Philippians 2:15).

4. Honesty confirms God's _____direction_____.

> *"Put away from you a deceitful mouth, and put devious lips far from you. Let your eyes look directly ahead. Watch the path of your feet, and all your ways will be established"* (Proverbs 4:24-26).

5. Even the smallest dishonesty is _____sin_____.

> *"Whoever is dishonest with very little will also be dishonest with much"* (Luke 16:10).

The people of God must be honest in even the smallest matters. Follow Abraham's example in Genesis 14:22-23.

> *"I have sworn to the Lord . . . that I will not take a thread or a sandal thong or anything that is yours."*

ESCAPING THE TEMPTATION TO BE DISHONEST

A healthy _____fear_____ of the Lord.

> *"By the fear of the Lord one keeps away from evil"* (Proverbs 16:6).

WHAT TO DO WHEN DISHONEST

1. Restore our fellowship with _____God_____.

> *"If we confess our sins, He is faithful and righteous to forgive us our sins and to cleanse us from all unrighteousness"* (1 John 1:9).

2. Return dishonest gain to its rightful _____owner_____.

> *"Then it shall be, when he sins and becomes guilty, that he shall restore what he took by robbery . . . he shall make restitution for it in full and add to it one-fifth more. He shall give it to the one to whom it belongs"* (Leviticus 6:4-5).

BLESSINGS AND CURSES

The Blessings for the Honest

1. Blessing of a more _____intimate_____ relationship with the Lord.

   "The Lord is . . . intimate with the upright" (Proverbs 3:32).

2. Blessing on the _____family_____

   "A righteous man who walks in his integrity—how blessed are his sons after him" (Proverbs 20:7).

3. Blessing of _____life_____

   "Truthful lips will be established forever, but a lying tongue is only for a moment" (Proverbs 12:19).

4. Blessing of _____abundance_____

   "Much wealth is in the house of the righteous, but trouble is the income of the wicked" (Proverbs 15:6).

The Curses on the Dishonest

1. Alienation from _____God_____

   "A crooked man is an abomination to the Lord" (Proverbs 3:32).

2. Trouble for the _____family_____

   "He who profits illicitly troubles his own house" (Proverbs 15:27).

3. Shorter Life-Span

   "The getting of treasures by a lying tongue is a fleeting vapor, the pursuit of death" (Proverbs 21:6).

4. Lack_____ of Abundance

   "Wealth obtained by fraud dwindles" (Proverbs 13:11).

The impact of _____one_____ honest person is truly significant.

> *"Roam to and fro through the streets of Jerusalem, and look now, and take note . . . if you can find a person, if there is one who does justice, who seeks truth, then I, the Lord, will pardon her"* (Jeremiah 5:1).

DISCUSSION QUESTIONS _____
(TIME)

1. Are you consistently honest in even the smallest details? If not, how do you propose to change?

2. What are two factors that motivate or influence us to act dishonestly?

   ■

   ■

3. Read *Proverbs 14:2*. Can you practice dishonesty and still love God? Why?

   [No, those who practice dishonesty hate God. The dishonest person acts as if the Lord does not exist.]

4. Read *Proverbs 26:28* and *Romans 13:9-10*. According to these passages, can you practice dishonesty and still love your neighbor? Why?

   [No, the dishonest person harms other people.]

PRAYER REQUESTS (OPTIONAL)

H O N E S T Y

DIG DEEPER AND LEARN MORE (OPTIONAL)

QUESTIONS TO ANSWER

1. Read *Leviticus 19:11-13*; *Deuteronomy 25:13-16*; and *Ephesians 4:25*. What do these verses communicate to you about God's demand for honesty?

   Leviticus 19:11-13— [The Lord commands us to be honest.]

   Deuteronomy 25:13-16— [The Lord demands honesty in our business dealings.]

   Ephesians 4:25— [We are not to lie to one another.]

2. Read *Exodus 18:21-22*. Does the Lord require honesty for leaders? Why?

   [The Lord requires honesty for leaders because they influence subordinates either for good or evil.]

3. Read *Exodus 22:1-4* and *Numbers 5:5-8*. What does the Bible say about restitution? If you have acquired anything dishonestly, what do you need to do?

   [Restitution is required.]

PRACTICAL EXERCISE TO COMPLETE

Recording your income and spending.
Many people are uneasy when considering a budget. A budget is often viewed as something that will mean a loss of freedom and endless hours of detailed accounting. But if properly understood and used, a budget can be enormously valuable for you. A budget is simply a plan for spending money.

The first step is to begin recording your income and spending to help you determine more accurately what you are actually earning and spending. This will be important to know later on when you complete the estimated budget.

RECORDING YOUR INCOME AND SPENDING

Date	Description	Amount of Spending	Amount of Income

HONESTY

RECORDING YOUR INCOME AND SPENDING

Date	Description	Amount of Spending	Amount of Income

CHAPTER FIVE

GIVING

"Remember the words of the Lord Jesus, that He Himself said, 'It is more blessed to give than to receive.'"
Acts 20:35

THE POOR WIDOW—
Gave everything she had.

THERE ARE FEW AREAS OF THE CHRISTIAN LIFE THAT CAN BE MORE fulfilling or exciting than the area of giving. Throughout the Bible we are encouraged to be generous and give. In fact, there are more verses related to giving than any other subject dealing with money.

Our heavenly Father is constantly giving to us, and He wants us to become conformed to His Son, Jesus Christ. Our giving is one of His ways to accomplish this goal.

ATTITUDE IN GIVING

Giving with the proper attitude is crucial.

> *"If I give all my possessions to feed the poor . . . but do not have love,
> it profits me ____nothing____ "* (1 Corinthians 13:3).

The Lord set the example of giving motivated by love.

> *"For God so ____loved____ the world, that He gave His only begotten
> Son"* (John 3:16).

GIVE TO GOD FIRST

> *"Honor the Lord from your wealth and from the ____first____ of all your
> produce"* (Proverbs 3:9).

Amount_____ TO GIVE

Giving a tithe (__10__ percent) of our income is the foundation.

> *"You have robbed Me of the tithes and offerings due Me. And so the awe-
> some curse of God is cursing you, for your whole nation has been robbing
> Me"* (Malachi 3:8, LB).

The New Testament builds on the foundation of tithes and offerings. Jesus
comends ____sacrificial____ giving.

ADVANTAGES OF GIVING

If a gift is given with the proper attitude, the giver benefits more than the
receiver.

> *"Remember the words of the Lord Jesus, that He Himself said, 'It is more
> ____blessed____ to give than to receive'"* (Acts 20:35).

CROWN FINANCIAL MINISTRIES

STUDIES FOR ALL AGES

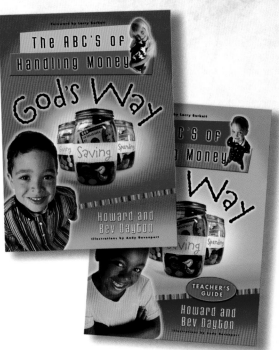

AGES 7 AND YOUNGER

This world teaches kids that money and possessions are a source of self-worth. Nothing could be farther from the truth. *The ABC's of Handling Money God's Way* is an excellent tool to combat these fallacies and teach children basic principles of working, giving, saving, and spending. This colorful, story-based workbook will engage children and keep them interested as they learn that God's plan for handling our finances is so much better than the world's way.

AGES 8 TO 12

Four children with a financial challenge learn the secret of giving, saving, spending, and much more. They also discover that they can trust God to provide. The principles are embedded in an exciting story of adventure that captures and holds the attention of children. *The Secret of Handling Money God's Way* is a colorful, story-based workbook that will engage children as they learn about God's plan for handling their finances.

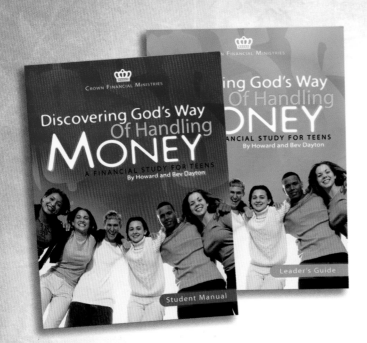

TEENS

Teens love this study! Besides memorizing a key Scripture and learning what God says about money, there is also a practical financial exercise at the end of each chapter. It is designed to help teens create habits that will set them on a lifelong journey of handling money responsibly.

ADULT SMALL GROUP STUDY

If you are interested in learning more about Crown's remarkably effective Small Group Study or if you want to introduce it to your church, order a set of the materials.

MONEY IN MARRIAGE

Statistics continue to show that at least 50 percent of all new marriages end in divorce; and, of the divorces surveyed, financial problems are given as the root cause in 80 percent of the cases. With the *Money in Marriage* CD-ROM software system, engaged or married couples of any age can benefit from the wisdom and practicality of this product.

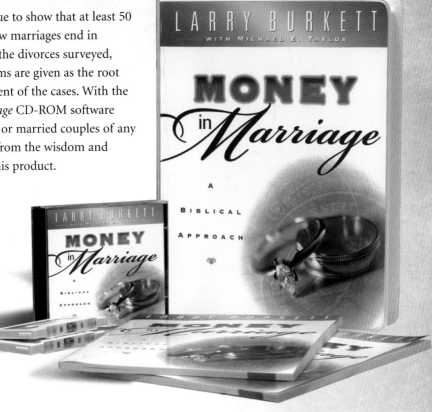

COLLEGIATE STUDY

College students are facing growing financial challenges, such as credit card debt and even gambling. Crown's Collegiate Edition is an excellent study to teach God's perspective of money to students at this formative time of their lives. It may be taught in a small group or college classroom.

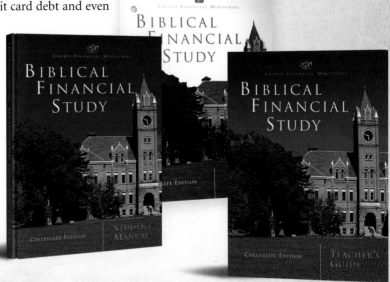

VIDEO TAPE SERIES

The *Discovering God's Way of Handling Money* video series is designed for a Sunday school class or a weekend seminar. A Course Workbook for students and a Leader's Guide accompany the video.

SET YOUR HOUSE IN ORDER

The *Set Your House in Order* workbook contains practically everything a person needs to plan his or her estate. Putting your financial house and estate in order is one of the most practical, thoughtful expressions of our care for our loved ones. This is also a wonderful gift to parents or grandparents.

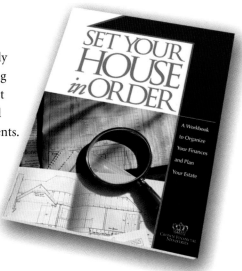

YOUR MONEY COUNTS— NOW A BOOK ON TAPE

Your Money Counts book or book on tape teaches the financial principles found in God's Word in an easily understood yet powerful way.

CROWN FINANCIAL
MINISTRIES

FOR MORE INFORMATION OR TO PLACE
AN ORDER, CALL 1-800-722-1976
OR VISIT US ONLINE
AT CROWN.ORG

1. Giving draws our _____hearts_____ toward Christ.

> *"For where your treasure is, there will your heart be also"* (Matthew 6:21).

2. Giving develops _____character_____.

3. Giving allows us to invest for _____eternity_____.

> *"But lay up for yourselves treasures in heaven . . ."* (Matthew 6:20).

4. Giving produces a _____material_____ increase to the giver.

> *"There is one who scatters, yet increases all the more, and there is one who withholds what is justly due, but it results only in want. The generous man will be prosperous, and he who waters will himself be watered"* (Proverbs 11:24).

To Whom Should We Give?

1. Our local _____church_____

Too many churches have been unable to effectively minister to their community and the world because of inadequate support.

2. Christian Ministries

3. The _____poor_____

> *"Lord when did we see You hungry, and feed You, or thirsty, and give You drink? . . . the King will answer and say, "To the extent you did it to one of these brothers of Mine, even the least of them, you did it to Me"* (Matthew 25:35-40).

Three areas of our Christian life are affected by giving to the poor.

1. Prayer

A lack of giving to the poor could be the cause of unanswered prayer.

> *"Divide your bread with the hungry and bring the homeless poor into the house . . . then you will call, and the Lord will answer"* (Isaiah 58:7-9).

2. Our _____provision_____

> *"He who gives to the poor will never want, but he who shuts his eyes will have many curses"* (Proverbs 28:27).

3. Knowing the Lord _____intimately_____

> *"'He pled the cause of the afflicted and needy; then it was well. Is not that what it means to know Me?' declares the Lord"* (Jeremiah 22:16).

Ask the Lord to bring one poor person into your life.

> *"I delivered the poor who cried for help, and the orphan who had no helper…I made the widow's heart sing for joy…I was eyes to the blind and feet to the lame. I was a father to the needy, and I investigated the case which I did not know"* (Job:29:12-16).

 # DISCUSSION QUESTIONS _____
(TIME)

1. What principle about giving in the video proved especially helpful or thought provoking?

2. Do you consistently give out of a heart of love? What is your attitude toward giving?

3. How do you think you can more effectively give to the poor?

 PRAYER REQUESTS (OPTIONAL)

DIG DEEPER AND LEARN MORE (OPTIONAL)

SCRIPTURE TO MEMORIZE
*"Remember the words of the Lord Jesus, that He Himself said,
'It is more blessed to give than to receive'"* (Acts 20:35).

QUESTIONS TO ANSWER

1. Read *Matthew 23:23* and *2 Corinthians 9:7*. What do each of these verses say about the importance of giving with the proper attitude? How can a person develop the proper attitude in giving?

   [Giving with the proper attitude is crucial. The only way to give out of a heart of love is to give each gift to Christ as an act of worship.]

2. Read *2 Corinthians 8:1-5*. Describe the principles from this passage that should influence how much you give.

   [They first gave themselves to the Lord.]

3. Read *Isaiah 58:6-11* and *Galatians 2:9-10*. What do these verses say about giving to the poor?

   [God protects us, answers our prayers and blesses us with joy when we give to the poor. The disciples had a deep concern for the needy.]

 ## PRACTICAL EXERCISE TO COMPLETE

The Estimated Monthly Budget (see next page) is one of the most important practical exercises of the entire study, and for many it proves to be the most difficult. You may be discouraged by what your estimated monthly budget reveals.

But keep heart—there is hope. Keep using and refining your budget until it balances.

ESTIMATED MONTHLY BUDGET

TOTAL MONTHLY INCOME   _____
    Salary   _____
    Interest and Dividends   _____
    Other Income   _____

EXPENSES

1. Tithe/Giving   _____

2. Taxes   _____

3. Housing   _____
    Mortgage or Rent   _____
    Insurance & Property Taxes   _____
    Utilities, Phone & Cable TV   _____
    Maintenance   _____
    Other   _____

4. Food   _____

5. Transportation   _____
    Payments   _____
    Gas, Oil & Repairs   _____
    Insurance/License   _____

6. Insurance   _____
    Life and Health   _____
    Other   _____

7. Debts   _____

GIVING

ESTIMATED MONTHLY BUDGET

8. Entertainment/Recreation   _____

9. Clothing   _____

10. Saving / Investments   _____

11. Medical Expenses   _____
    Doctor and Dentist   _____
    Prescriptions   _____
    Other   _____

12. Miscellaneous   _____
    Toiletries/Cosmetics   _____
    Laundry/Cleaning   _____
    Gifts (incl.Christmas)   _____
    Tuition and materials   _____
    Day Care   _____
    Other   _____

TOTAL EXPENSES   _____

INCOME VS. LIVING EXPENSES:

Total Income   _____

Minus Total Expenses   _____

Monthly Surplus or Deficit   ========

GIVING

CHAPTER SIX

WORK

*"Whatever you do, do your work
heartily, as for the Lord rather than
for men . . . It is the Lord Christ
whom you serve."*
Colossians 3:23, 24

LYDIA—
A seller of purple fabric.

FEW PEOPLE ARE COMPLETELY SATISFIED WITH THEIR JOBS. BORE-
dom, lack of fulfillment, fear of losing a job, inadequate wages,
and countless other pressures contribute to a high level of
discontentment. The frustrations are similar for all professions includ-
ing doctors, homemakers, salespeople, and blue-collar workers.

During a 50-year career the average person spends 100,000
hours working. Unfortunately, many just endure their work while
ignoring the fact that 25 percent of their lives is devoted to a
distasteful job. On the other hand, some people like work so much
that they neglect the other priorities of life.

In order to find satisfaction in our work, we need to understand
what Scripture teaches about it.

GOD CREATED WORK

> *"The Lord God took the man and put him into the garden of Eden to cultivate it and keep it"* (Genesis 2:15).

The very first thing the Lord did with Adam was to assign him work. After the Fall, work was made more difficult.

> *"Cursed is the ground because of you; in toil you shall eat of it all the days of your life. Both thorns and thistles it shall grow for you; and you shall eat the plants of the field; by the sweat of your face you shall eat bread"* (Genesis 3:17).

GOD'S PERSPECTIVE ON WORK

1. Work is necessary.

> *"If anyone will not ____work____, neither let him eat"* (2 Thessalonians 3:10).

2. Work develops ____character____.

3. We should work for the Lord.

> *"Whatever you do, do your work heartily, as for the Lord rather than for men . . . It is the Lord Christ whom you serve"* (Colossians 3:23, 24).

4. There is ____equal____ dignity in all types of work.

Scripture does not elevate any honest profession above another.

THE LORD'S RESPONSIBILITIES IN WORK

1. God gives us our job ____skills____.

> *"And every skillful person in whom the Lord has put skill and understanding to know how to perform all the work"* (Exodus 36:1).

W O R K

2. God gives us our _____success_____.

"The Lord was with Joseph, so he became a successful man . . . his master saw that the Lord was with him and how the Lord caused all that he did to prosper in his hand" (Genesis 39:2, 3).

3. God controls our ____promotion____.

"For promotion and power come from nowhere on earth, but only from God" (Psalm 75:6, LB).

OUR RESPONSIBILITIES IN WORK

1. We should work _____hard_____.

"Whatever your hand finds to do, do it with all your might" (Ecclesiastes 9:10).

"The precious posession of a man is ____diligence____" (Proverbs 12:27)

Your work should be at such a level that people will never equate laziness with God.

2. We should not overwork.

"You shall work six days, but on the seventh day you shall rest; even during plowing time and harvest you shall rest" (Exodus 34:21).

RESPONSIBILITIES OF A GODLY EMPLOYEE

1. Absolute _____honesty_____

"No evidence of corruption" (Daniel 6:4).

2. Faithful_____

"He [Daniel] was faithful" (Daniel 6:4).

3. Prayer

"Now when Daniel knew that the document was signed . . . he continued kneeling on his knees three times a day, ____praying____ and giving thanks before his God, as he had been doing previously" (Daniel 6:10).

W O R K

4. Honoring your ___employer___

> *"Servants* [employees], *be submissive to your masters* [employer] *with all respect, not only to those who are good and gentle, but also to those who are unreasonable"* (1 Peter 2:18).

5. Honoring fellow ___employees___

Never slander a fellow employee.

6. ___Sharing___ our faith

 ## DISCUSSION QUESTIONS _____
(TIME)

1. Do you work hard? If not, describe what steps you will take to improve your work habits.

2. What are the things that keep you from working hard?

3. Do you work too hard? How will you guard against overwork?

4. How will you apply what you learned about work?

 ## PRAYER REQUESTS (OPTIONAL)

 ## DIG DEEPER AND LEARN MORE (OPTIONAL)

 ### SCRIPTURE TO MEMORIZE
> *"Whatever you do, do your work heartily, as for the Lord rather than for men . . . It is the Lord Christ whom you serve"* (Colossians 3:23-24).

QUESTIONS TO ANSWER

1. Read *Colossians 3:22-25*. For whom do you really work? How will this understanding alter your work performance?

   [We work for Christ.]

2. Read *Exodus 34:21*. What does this communicate to you about rest? Do you get sufficient rest?

   [Hard work should be balanced with adequate rest.]

3. Is it biblically permissible for a person to retire, only to pursue a life of leisure? If so, what passages in the Bible supports this kind of retirement?

   [It is not biblically permissible to retire to a life of leisure. We should strive to be productive as long as we are physically able.]

 PRACTICAL EXERCISE TO COMPLETE

When you completed your Estimated Monthly Budget and subtracted your spending from your income, did you have more income than spending? Many people discover that their current spending adds up to more than their income.

Your assignment this session is to adjust and balance your budget. Are there creative ways you can increase your income? Carefully review each spending category and ask yourself: Do I really need this? Or can I purchase it for less?

It is not easy to reduce spending, and some of the decisions may be difficult. It may be necessary to consider a change in housing, automobiles, insurance, private schools, cable television, and so forth. The objective is to balance your budget.

Now, go back to the Estimated Monthly Budget and prayerfully consider what changes are necessary to balance your budget.

CHAPTER SEVEN

SAVING AND INVESTING

"Steady plodding brings prosperity."

JOSEPH—
Saved during the seven years
of plenty.

MANY PEOPLE IN OUR COUNTRY ARE NOT CONSISTENT SAVERS. The average person saves less than one percent of their income and 35 percent of all adults have *no savings* whatsoever. This is contrary to Scripture which encourages us to save.

VIDEO NOTES _____
(TIME)

IT IS WISE TO SAVE.

"The wise man _____saves_____ for the future, but the foolish man spends whatever he gets" (Proverbs 21:20, LB).

Saving means to forego an expenditure today so you will have something to spend in the future.

When you receive income, the first check you write should be a gift to the Lord and the second check to your _____savings_____.

METHODS OF SAVINGS

- Income from tax refunds or bonuses
- A certain percentage
- Automatic savings plan available through banks or work

INVESTMENT PRINCIPLES

1. Be a _____steady_____ plodder.

   "Steady plodding brings prosperity; hasty speculation brings poverty" (Proverbs 21:5, LB).

The fundamental principle you need to practice to become a successful investor is to spend less than you earn. Then save and invest the difference over a long period of time.

2. Let __compounding__ work for you.

There are three variables in compounding:

- The ____amount____ you save.
- The percent return you earn on your savings.
- The length of time you save.

Be like the ants!

   "Four things on earth are small, yet they are extremely wise: ants are creatures of little strength, yet they store up their food in the summer" (Proverbs 30:24, 25, NIV).

3. Avoid _____risky_____ investments.

   "There is another serious problem I have seen everywhere—savings are put into risky investments that turn sour, and soon there is nothing left to pass on to one's son. The man who speculates is soon back to where he began— with nothing" (Ecclesiastes 5:13, 14, LB).

GAMBLING

The Bible does not specifically prohibit gambling; however, many who gamble do so in an attempt to get rich quickly. This is a violation of Scripture.

Make a commitment never to participate in gambling or lotteries even for entertainment. We should not expose ourselves to the risk of becoming compulsive gamblers, nor should we support an industry that enslaves so many.

4. Diversify _____.

> *"Divide your portion to seven, or even to eight, for you do not know what misfortune may occur on the earth"* (Ecclesiastes 11:2).

There is no investment without risk, and Scripture does not recommend any specific investments.

5. Count _____ the cost.

With every investment there are costs: financial costs, time commitments and efforts required.

Save and Invest Only When Also Giving.

Jesus called the rich man a fool (in Luke 12:16-21) because he saved _____ all _____ of his goods.

ACCEPTABLE GOALS FOR INVESTING

1. To provide for your _____ family _____.

> *"If any one does not provide for his own, and especially for those of his household, he has denied the faith and is worse than an unbeliever"* (1 Timothy 5:8).

2. To diminish _____ dependence _____ upon salary.

The more savings produce, the less dependent upon income from work.

3. To accumulate capital to operate business without _____ debt _____.

You Can Know God

1. God _____loves_____ you.

The Lord has a wonderful plan for your life and wants you to know Him.

> *"God so loved the world, that He gave His only begotten Son, that whoever believes in Him shall not perish, but have eternal life"* (John 3:16).

2. Unfortunately, we are _____separated_____ from God.

God is holy and He will not have a relationship with anyone who also is not perfect. Sadly, every person has sinned, and the consequence of sin is separation from God.

> *"For all have sinned and fall short of the glory of God"* (Romans 3:23).

This diagram illustrates our separation from God:

3. Jesus Christ is the only _____answer_____ to the separation problem.

Jesus Christ died on the cross to pay the penalty for our sin and bridge the gap between God and us.

> *"Jesus said . . . 'I am the way, and the truth, and the life; no one comes to the Father but through Me'"* (John 14:6).

> *"For the wages of sin is death, but the free gift of God is eternal life in Christ Jesus our Lord"* (Romans 6:23).

4. We can _____choose_____ to acccept Jesus Christ.

"For by grace you have been saved through faith; and that not of yourselves, it is the gift of God; not as a result of works, that no one should boast" (Ephesians 2:8-9).

I have a choice—accept Him, open the door of my heart or do nothing and reject Him.

"Behold I stand at the door and knock; if anyone hears My voice and opens the door, I will come in to him, and will dine with him, and he with Me" (Revelation 3:20).

If you desire to know the Lord and are not certain whether you have this relationship, you may ask Christ to come into your life and settle this issue by repeating this simple prayer. "Father God, I need You. I invite Jesus to come into my life and make me the person You want me to be. Thank You for forgiving my sins and giving me the gift of eternal life."

Please contact Crown Ministries if we can answer any questions or help you in any way.

DISCUSSION QUESTIONS _____ (TIME)

1. Are you a consistent saver? If so, share what methods you use to save.

2. If you have not saved regularly, what steps will you take to begin? (Remember, even if you can only save a small amount, begin this habit.)

3. What are your saving and investing goals? Are they scripturally permissible?

4. The Bible cautions us against risky investments. What steps can you take that will help protect you against risky investments?

PRAYER REQUESTS (OPTIONAL)

DIG DEEPER AND LEARN MORE (OPTIONAL)

SCRIPTURE TO MEMORIZE
"The wise man saves for the future, but the foolish man spends whatever he gets" (Proverbs 21:20, LB).

QUESTIONS TO ANSWER

1. Read *Genesis 41:34-36; Proverbs 21:20* and *Proverbs 30:24-25* and answer:

   What do these passages communicate about savings?

   Genesis 41:34-36 — [Joseph saved for a future need.]

   Proverbs 21:20 — [The wise save, but the foolish only consume.]

   Proverbs 30:24-25 — [Ants are commended because they save.]

2. Read *Luke 12:16-21, 34.*

   Why did the Lord call the rich man a fool?
   [Because he saved everything.]

   According to this parable, why do you think it is scripturally permissible to save only when you are also giving?
   [Only when we give can our hearts be drawn to the Lord.]

3. Carefully think about your saving and investing goals. Describe what you will need to do to accomplish these goals?

4. What steps will you take next week that will help you make progress toward reaching your goals?

 **PRACTICAL EXERCISE TO COMPLETE**

You are now ready to begin your budget.

On the first line of the Monthy Budget Form (see next page) insert the budgeted amounts for your monthly income and your spending in each of the 12 expense categories.

- Whenever you receive income or spend money during the month, note that amount in the appropriate day and column.

- At the end of the month, add each column and compare the actual income and spending with the amounts budgeted.

- Add all the expenses together and subtract this figure from the total income to compute your surplus or deficit.

- Carefully review each spending category every month to determine whether you are consistently overspending in a category that may require adjustment in your estimated budget.

Would you prefer to use a computer to track your budget's income and expenses? Crown Financial Ministries has an excellent software tool called *Money Matters* that will help you plan, budget, and manage your family's finances according to biblical principles.

BUDGET FOR THE MONTH OF _____

BUDGET DAY	Income	Giving	Taxes	Housing	Food	Trans.	Insurance	Debt	Enter.	Clothing	Saving	Medical	Misc.
1													
2													
3													
4													
5													
6													
7													
8													
9													
10													
11													
12													
13													
14													
15													
16													
17													
18													
19													
20													
21													
22													
23													
24													
25													
26													
27													
28													
29													
30													
31													
TOTALS													
± BUDGET													

Income: _____   Less Total Expenses: _____   Surplus or Deficit: _____

BUDGET FOR THE MONTH OF _____

BUDGET DAY	Income	Giving	Taxes	Housing	Food	Trans.	Insurance	Debt	Enter.	Clothing	Saving	Medical	Misc.
1													
2													
3													
4													
5													
6													
7													
8													
9													
10													
11													
12													
13													
14													
15													
16													
17													
18													
19													
20													
21													
22													
23													
24													
25													
26													
27													
28													
29													
30													
31													
TOTALS													
± BUDGET													

Income: _____   Less Total Expenses: _____   Surplus or Deficit: _____

BUDGET FOR THE MONTH OF _____

BUDGET DAY	Income	Giving	Taxes	Housing	Food	Trans.	Insurance	Debt	Enter.	Clothing	Saving	Medical	Misc.
1													
2													
3													
4													
5													
6													
7													
8													
9													
10													
11													
12													
13													
14													
15													
16													
17													
18													
19													
20													
21													
22													
23													
24													
25													
26													
27													
28													
29													
30													
31													
TOTALS													
± BUDGET													

Income: _____   Less Total Expenses: _____   Surplus or Deficit: _____

BUDGET FOR THE MONTH OF _____

DAY	Income	Giving	Taxes	Housing	Food	Trans.	Insurance	Debt	Enter.	Clothing	Saving	Medical	Misc.
1													
2													
3													
4													
5													
6													
7													
8													
9													
10													
11													
12													
13													
14													
15													
16													
17													
18													
19													
20													
21													
22													
23													
24													
25													
26													
27													
28													
29													
30													
31													
TOTALS													
± BUDGET													

Income: _____ Less Total Expenses: _____ Surplus or Deficit: _____

BUDGET FOR THE MONTH OF _____

BUDGET DAY	Income	Giving	Taxes	Housing	Food	Trans.	Insurance	Debt	Enter	Clothing	Saving	Medical	Misc.
1													
2													
3													
4													
5													
6													
7													
8													
9													
10													
11													
12													
13													
14													
15													
16													
17													
18													
19													
20													
21													
22													
23													
24													
25													
26													
27													
28													
29													
30													
31													
TOTALS													
± BUDGET													

Income: _____   Less Total Expenses: _____   Surplus or Deficit: _____

CHAPTER EIGHT

CHILDREN

*"Train up a child in the way he
should go, even when he is old
he will not depart from it."*
Proverbs 22:6

LEARNING TO HANDLE MONEY IS PART OF A CHILD'S EDUCATION, A
part that parents cannot leave to teachers. They must direct it
themselves because spending experiences are found in the outside
world rather than in the classroom.

How well prepared were you to make financial decisions when
you left home? Parents and teachers spend 18 to 22 years prepar-
ing youth for occupations but generally less than a few hours
teaching children the value and use of the money they will earn
during their careers. Each generation has the responsibility to
leave their children the legacy of understanding and applying
God's financial principles.

VIDEO NOTES _____
(TIME)

CROWN MINISTRIES CHILDREN'S STUDIES

Teens Study

The Secret— for children ages 8 to 12

The ABC's of Handling Money God's Way— for children ages 7 and younger

The studies may be taught one-on-one, in small groups, in a Sunday school class or in a school setting. No special training is required to teach these studies. A helpful leader's guide is available for each study.

PARENTS' RESPONSIBLITY

1. Verbal _____ Communication

> *"And these words, which I am commanding you today, shall be on your heart; and you shall teach them diligently to your sons and shall talk of them when you sit in your house and when you walk by the way and when you lie down and when you rise up"* (Deuteronomy 6:6, 7).

2. Model _____ Financial Faithfulness

> *"Be imitators of me, just as I also am of Christ"* (1 Corinthians 11:1).

God the Father sent the perfect model, Jesus Christ, to demonstrate how we should live.

> *"Everyone, after he has been fully trained, will be like his teacher"* (Luke 6:40).

We can teach what we believe, but we only _____ reproduce _____ who we are.

3. Create Learning Opportunities

TEACHING CHILDREN HOW TO MANAGE MONEY

1. Budgeting

As soon as the child is ready for school, he or she should begin to receive an _____income_____ to manage.

Parents should establish _____boundaries_____ and offer advice on how to spend money, but children must have freedom of choice.

When children begin to receive an income, teach them how to _____budget_____.

2. Giving

3. Saving

The habit of _____saving_____ should be established as soon as the child receives an income.

Teach your children the benefits of _____compounding_____ interest.

4. Debt

Teach them how difficult it is to get out of _____debt_____.

TEACHING CHILDREN TO _____work_____

The best way for a child to become faithful in work is to establish the habit of daily _____household_____ chores.

The objective of training your child in the value of work is to build _____character_____.

STRATEGY FOR _____independence_____

Each child independently managing all of his or her own finances—with the exception of food and shelter—by their senior year in high school.

_____grandparents_____ can play a key role in helping to train children.

DISCUSSION QUESTIONS (TIME)

1. How well prepared were you to handle money when you left home? What financial areas did you understand well? Why?

2. Are you modeling wise money management to your children and grandchildren. If not, what will you do?

3. Describe how you are training your children or grandchildren to give generously, save consistently, and spend wisely. If you have not yet begun to train them, how will you begin?

4. What are you doing to teach them the value of working hard?

 PRAYER REQUESTS (OPTIONAL)

 DIG DEEPER AND LEARN MORE (OPTIONAL)

 SCRIPTURE TO MEMORIZE
"Train up a child in the way he should go, even when he is old he will not depart from it" (Proverbs 22:6).

1. Read *Deuteronomy 6:6-7* and *Deuteronomy 11:18-19*. According to these passages, who is responsible for teaching children the biblical perspective of handling money?

   [It is the responsibility of parents.]

2. Describe how you are going to teach children to be generous givers.

3. List five practical ideas for teaching children how to become wise spenders.

4. What are some effective methods for teaching children to work hard and to work "as unto the Lord?"

 PRACTICAL EXERCISE TO COMPLETE

Most children have not been taught God's way of handling money. As an unfortunate consequence, children leave home ill-equipped to manage their financial future. This lesson's practical application is designed as a checklist to help you train children to earn and manage money from a biblical perspective.

TEACHING CHILDREN TO HANDLE MONEY

Income
- Are your children receiving an income?
- Are they performing routine chores around the home in return for their income?

Budgeting
- Are your children budgeting?
- Describe the method they are using to budget.

Saving and Investing
- Is there a savings account opened in the name of your child?
- Have you taught your children the concept of compound interest?
- Describe what your children know about investments.

Debt
- Have you taught your children the biblical principles dealing with debt?
- Are they aware of the true cost of interest?

Giving
- Have you taught your children the principles of giving?
- Describe their giving.

Work
- Do your children understand the biblical perspective of work?
- Describe the jobs your children perform for others to earn money.

PRAYER
REQUESTS

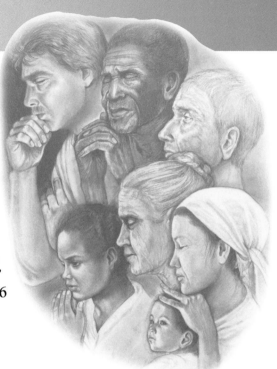

*"Pray for one another . . . the
effective prayer of a righteous
man can accomplish much."*
James 5:16

BEFORE YOU END YOUR CLASS EACH WEEK, YOU MAY WANT TO
take prayer requests. There is one page for each chapter for you
to record these requests. Please consider praying daily for those
in your class.

CHAPTER 1 PRAYER REQUESTS

Date	Person	Prayer Request(s)

CHAPTER 2 PRAYER REQUESTS

Date	Person	Prayer Request(s)

CHAPTER 3 PRAYER REQUESTS

Date	Person	Prayer Request(s)

PRAYER REQUESTS

CHAPTER 4 PRAYER REQUESTS

Date	Person	Prayer Request(s)

CHAPTER 5 PRAYER REQUESTS

Date	Person	Prayer Request(s)

CHAPTER 6 PRAYER REQUESTS

Date	Person	Prayer Request(s)

CHAPTER 7 PRAYER REQUESTS

Date	Person	Prayer Request(s)

CHAPTER 8 PRAYER REQUESTS

Date	Person	Prayer Request(s)